Get It Right
This Time™

Dear Carmen,
Lead with your mind and follow your heart!
Warmly
Amy

2/13

Get It Right This Time™

How to Find and Keep
Your Ideal Romantic Relationship

Amy Schoen, MBA, CPCC

Heartmind Connection®, LLC
ROCKVILLE, MARYLAND

Although the author and publisher have made every effort to ensure the
accuracy and completeness of information contained in this book, we assume
no responsibility for errors, inaccuracies, omissions, or any inconsistency herein.
Any slighting of people, places, or organizations is unintentional.

First printing 2008

ISBN 978-0-9795130-1-5
LCCN 2007931507

**ATTENTION CORPORATIONS, UNIVERSITIES, COLLEGES, AND
PROFESSIONAL ORGANIZATIONS:** Quantity discounts are available on bulk
purchases of this book for educational, gift purposes, or as premiums for increasing
magazine subscriptions or renewals. Special books or book excerpts can also be
created to fit specific needs. For information, please contact
Heartmind Connection®, LLC, 10423 Englishman Drive,
Rockville, MD 20852; (240) 498-7803.

♥ ♥ ♥

To my mother, Marlene,
who taught me to focus on what I want,
to persevere, and not to give up!

To my husband, Alan,
who gave me the opportunity to grow
and learn through our love.

Table of Contents

Part I

The Get It Right This Time™ Method

*Here you are…*single again! This is not what you had expected at this point in your life. So what are your choices now? To give up? To change your career focus? To concentrate on your tennis game instead of your love life? Why not pick yourself up and try again? Perhaps you will Get It Right This Time™!

I know how hard it is to try again, having gone through a divorce at age thirty-six after eleven years of marriage. Most of us don't go into relationships expecting them to fail. My own personal journey inspired me to do the research and to collect the information contained in this book. Fortunately, I found happiness with a wonderful man—my second husband—using many of the approaches and strategies that are outlined for you in this book, thereby providing you with the benefit of my experience.

The main goal with this book is to help others who are struggling with dating and relationships and to make it easier to succeed in love. Finding myself single again in my mid-thirties, I became tenacious about seeking knowledge about relationships by reading books, attending seminars, joining support groups (I became a member of New Beginnings, a group for separated and divorced individuals in the Washington, D.C. area) and working with a coach. I was determined to Get It Right This Time™!

It became evident to me that there are tons of useful information out there for those who have survived a failed relationship. With that information gathered into this concise book, you have the benefit of my experience and wisdom at your fingertips to make a better choice for yourself this time. By reading about how others have tried and failed, you may be able to avoid the same pitfalls. As the saying goes, "Those who do not learn from the past are doomed to repeat it."

Look at each relationship in your quest for love as a feedback loop of useful information. You can learn not only from websites, books, and CDs but also from experiencing things that help you refine your dating approach. By learning how to select more appropriate people and by frequenting the places where you are able to connect with "like people", you will improve your chances of meeting and dating with success. You will eventually be successful, as I was. I met my husband at age forty-one and married at age forty-two—where marriage was my goal. Believe me, the process of dating got weary at times. But I persevered. This book is a compilation of perspectives about people who date and the dating process itself. It will provide useful advice to an audience desperately seeking a better way to date and wanting to get off the dating merry-go-round. The main theme of the book is that experience is our teacher. Don't give up. The next person could be The Right One.

It's important to stay positive about yourself and the dating process. When you do, you give yourself a better chance to succeed. Many of my clients come to me in despair. They were not expecting to be alone at this time in their lives. Many have disappointed dreams of not having the relationship or family they wanted. They have almost given up hope. As the relationship coach, I am on their sidelines cheering my clients on with, "You can do it! You can find the right romantic relationship if you stick with the race!"

Dating is a marathon—you've got to keep on going to get to the finish line. Everyone has something attractive to another individual.

You have your positive attributes or your "THRIVE" (Talents-Heart-Reasons-Interests-Values-Energy). Therefore, another key message of the book is to focus on what you do have to offer instead of what you do not have—to put your own personal beauty out there in the universe in ways to meet people who will appreciate you for you.

Ideally, this book will become your personal coach to give you reinforcement when things seem rough out there in the dating arena. Let it give you inspiration to pick yourself up and try again. Let it encourage you to refine your approach by learning what works for you and what doesn't. Let it challenge you to try new ways to meet The Right One. So get out there, because today could be the day you find true love and Get It Right This Time™!

Are You Ready for The Right One?

Find out by taking this quiz! (Please answer honestly)

1. Do you feel you are in a good place in your life with your career?   YES   NO

2. Do you feel that the single's dating scene is getting tiring and stale?   YES   NO

3. Do you have a good understanding of yourself and what your needs are in a relationship?   YES   NO

4. Do you have a sense of what kind of person would be the ideal partner for you?   YES   NO

5. Do you know how you feel about children?   YES   NO

6. Do you plan your weekly activities with the goal of meeting someone to date?   YES   NO

7. Are you realistic about the give-and-take needed in a relationship, and are you prepared to give?   YES   NO

8. Are you willing to change an aspect of your life to accommodate your partner (such as moving to the next town or another state and changing jobs)?   YES   NO

9. Do you commit five to ten hours a week to activities that will enable you to meet a potential partner such as the Internet, singles events, and other social activities?   YES   NO

10. Have you taken a seminar or read a book to learn how to improve your knowledge of dating and relationships in order to have better success?   YES   NO

11. Have you improved your image lately to present the best and most desirable *you* possible?   YES   NO

12. Are you looking to meet a person who meets your non-negotiable needs rather than relying solely on chemistry?   YES   NO

13. Have you consulted with a therapist or dating coach in the last three years in order to help you learn how to be more successful with dating and how to establish a long-term relationship?   YES   NO

14. Have you disclosed to your friends, family, and acquaintances that you are looking to meet someone to date and would appreciate being set up?   YES   NO

15. Have you signed up for a dating or introduction service this year?   YES   NO

16. Is finding a life partner in the top three priorities in your life to accomplish this year?   YES   NO

Scoring

13 to 16 YES: You are very ready to meet The Right One. You are on your way to meeting your life's love partner very soon. Keep at it, your beloved is right around the corner!

6 to 12 YES: You are somewhat ready to meet your life's love partner. You may be having too much fun dating and not be so serious about settling down with one person. You probably have other priorities in your life that are more important at the moment than meeting The Right One.

Fewer than 6 YES: You are not ready for meeting The Right One. You are not in a frame of mind to put this aspect of your life on the top of your list. You may be clueless about who would be best suited for you. This person could even be in your life right now and you would not have the foresight to recognize it!

Part II

Who Are You?

Here's what you need to know about yourself before you seek a serious partnership.

Your Values, Life Goals, and Must-Haves

Many people don't know how to be honest with themselves about themselves. They know what they weigh, how many children (or cats) they have, and how much money they make, but they have never thought about how they might appear to another person, especially a person who is searching for a partner. Here's a way of checking yourself out. Ask yourself: What are my concerns, my loyalties, my ideals?

What Are My Values?

Loyalties

- Caring for my family
- Supporting my friends

Concerns

- Preserving my health
- Compassion for animals
- Community service

Ideals

- Political awareness
- Environmental stewardship
- Personal growth

What Are My Goals?

Ask yourself: If I had all the money in the world and nothing to stop me (like family obligations, job responsibilities, health issues) what would I want to do?

What Are My Must-Haves?

Finally, make a list of your must-haves in life and in your relationships. What are the things you will not negotiate with another person about—because they are so important to you? What is most valuable to you?

❤ Coach Amy's Dating Wisdom

Visualize yourself in the relationship you want. Pick a date, think up your ideal partner, close your eyes, and see yourself together with that person. However, acting "as if" you will find the right relationship is not enough. You must believe that the person you want is out there and looking for you. My clients who can get past the "as if" stage and truly *believe* that the ideal relationship is in store for them end up finding The One much faster.

The Non-Negotiable Must-Haves

Here are the Big Six Must-Haves I've found in my coaching business:

1. *Living space.* Some people don't want to live with a slob whereas others cringe at the thought of living with a neatnik. An old-house-do-it-yourselfer isn't going to be comfortable in a sleek condo.

2. *Pets.* Cockatiels, fish tanks, mynah birds, Chihuahuas, black labs, white mice, and pampered Persians: You love them or you hate them. Allergies, cat hair everywhere, and always having to walk the dog can make pets a deal breaker.

3. *City of residence.* If he wants to live in Louisiana and she wants to stay in L.A., it's not going to work. If she loves the garden she keeps in the burbs and he likes skating at midnight through the streets of San Francisco, the relationship is not going to pan out.

4. *Hobbies.* If you are a triathlete who trains four times a week, you may want to find someone who can share the experience. Or you may be drawn to someone who will enjoy the breathing space your time away at the track provides.

5. *Idea of fun.* The macrobiotic meditator is going to have a hard time with a partner who spends Sunday afternoons throwing back beers at the sports bar. Like to smoke a little reefer and listen to Miles Davis? You're not going to get along with a partner who gets high on fresh air and five-mile hikes. Dating is a great way to discover how a potential partner unwinds, parties, and spends time with friends.

6. *Smoking.* With smoking taboo in most public spaces these days, the 20% percent of Americans who still smoke will want to light up at home, in private times. Can you stand it? If you can't, is the smoking partner ready to give it up for you?

By knowing your must-haves, you will be able to skip over dating people who do not meet your real needs. This will save you time and heartache in the long run.

What Are Your Relationship Roadblocks?

There are two kinds of roadblocks: the ones we set up for ourselves and the ones others set up in our path.

Internal Roadblocks: False Beliefs We Keep

Lack of Confidence. Do you think you can't date because you are too short or not rich enough? If you do, you are only human! Most of us do have shortcomings that we are very aware of. However, you can choose *not* to listen to the voices in your head taunting you for your faults. This determines your ability to succeed in the dating world. What are you saying to yourself in order to sabotage your dating success?

There's No Point in Trying to Date. Or maybe you are convinced there are no nice women or reliable men anyway, so why bother? With the divorce rate where it's at—50% of all first relationships and over 60% of second relationships—there are always nice women and reliable men coming on the scene. They want to settle down; they want to Get It Right This Time™. So, what's holding you back?

Most Romantic Relationships Are Traps and Usually Fail. Our view of a relationship is based on those of other people—parents and close relatives, our parents' friends, and our own friends—that we have seen throughout our lives. Our past experiences—and prior relationships—have affected our perspective on what a relationship can be. Many who have been through difficult divorces would view a relationship as "painful" and a spouse as a "ball-and-chain." Since experience has formed this negative idea of a relationship, try gathering some positive experiences by reading about Ronald and Nancy Reagan, Goldie Hawn and Kurt Russell, or Paul Newman and Joanne Woodward, or hanging out with that happy couple who lives next door.

External Roadblocks: Life Circumstances That Tend to Limit Us

There can be practical life circumstances that are preventing you from dating and having a fulfilling relationship leading to something permanent. You may think you have no control over these. Do any of these statements sound familiar?

- I prefer that my last child graduate from high school and move out of the house before I can think about a serious relationship.
- My finances are finally in order. I can't afford to take on the additional expenses of dating.

- My job requires me to travel out of town more than half the time during the week.
- My job is very demanding, so I work seventy hours a week. I have no time for a relationship.
- My parents are very old, and I need to care for them.
- My friends and my partner don't get along all that well.
- My family doesn't approve of my partner.

If any of these seem familiar, ask yourself: What changes in my life can I make in order to give myself a better opportunity to date, or for relationship success?

Part III

Study Dating Like You Would the Stock Market

As you prepare yourself for dating, it's important to figure out the true reasons people are dating. People date for many different reasons. Just as a stock picker tries to understand why a certain stock is going up, so you want to understand why the person you are dating is going out with you. Is it to have a great time? To meet new people? To enjoy sports or music with another person? To share activities like walking or dancing? Or to find a lifelong relationship?

Why Do People Date?
What Are Their Real Reasons for Dating?

Just about every dater does want companionship. This is the number one reason most daters give. Here are some of the other reasons people date:

- *To share common interests with someone.* In this category, a dater might be interested in a golf partner or a fellow opera buff. The relationship is limited to one activity—like playing golf or hearing opera—and does not lead to a more committed relationship.

- *To have sex, period!* These single-minded daters are looking for one thing. Relationships with them will not deepen because they will always be looking for new conquests.

23

- *To find a steady partner and escape from the endless round of dating.* This is not a step toward commitment; it's simply an avoidance of dating. This man or woman wants someone around so he or she doesn't have to deal with strangers and prefers to be in a comfortable relationship.
- *To have fun—going to movies, eating out, rollerblading.* These people like to share activities that they would be doing anyway. Forming a long-term relationship is not their priority.
- *To meet new people for fun times, for business, or just out of curiosity about the world.* This dater is usually living for the moment and might even find a steady relationship confining.
- *To find someone who wants to have a family.*
- *To find a close relationship.* These people are looking for someone who shares that preference.
- *To find personal security.* Some people want a relationship in order not to be alone. They feel safe having a partner living with them and vulnerable when they are alone.
- *To achieve a particular lifestyle and economic security.* Some daters see a committed relationship as a way of getting a better life. For instance, a woman in this category might not want to work anymore and might look for a husband for financial support. A man in this category might feel less financial pressure in a marriage to a woman who has a steady job.
- *To find someone who believes in him or her, someone who inspires and offers emotional support.* This dater is often ambitious and wants to share living life at its fullest. These daters are usually interested in personal growth.
- *To get to know someone to share an intimate long-term relationship or marriage.* For this dater, having children and starting a family are not in the picture. Sometimes daters in this category already have children; sometimes they do not want them. They like the intimacy of a close relationship.

Study the intentions of the people you date, and be aware when your aims and theirs are not the same. This will save you precious time, as well as heartache.

Are You Attracting Others?
Positive Versus Negative Vibes

When you first meet a potential partner, it is best to keep the focus on the other person and not on yourself. Nonetheless, you may want to identify your strong points and really strut them. If you're not clear about what your strong points are, ask a friend or relative to tell you. You don't want to come across as cocky or arrogant, but you don't want to be mousy either. Be self-assured by giving off positive vibrations about yourself and about the other person, and you will move the relationship forward.

Positive
- Smiling
- Being responsive to others
- Asking about others
- Providing spontaneous answers
- Putting a positive spin on events
- Maintaining an understated presence
- Speaking in a low voice, warm tone
- Being free with compliments

Negative
- Having a flat expression or mouth turned down
- Looking down, avoiding eye contact
- Straining for attention
- Answering with abrupt, one-word responses
- Making critical comments
- Calling attention to oneself
- Being nervous and speaking too loudly
- Always complaining

A good example of someone who has a negative aura about her is my friend Kate, whom I invited to my wedding. She looked miserable the whole time as if she had a black cloud over her head—that was surely a turnoff. If only she had made the best of the experience—there were many single guys to meet at my wedding.

To make sure you are following on track with the Get It Right This Time™ method to dating and relationships: Download a copy of the Get It Right This Time Worksheet by visiting my website www.GetItRightThisTime.com/worksheet.html.

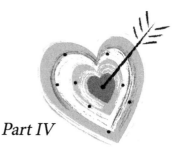

Part IV

Preparing for
Get It Right Dating

Like any endeavor in life, success depends upon preparation. Put yourself in the frame of mind for success. Find people to support you and ways to increase your chances for successfully meeting The Right One.

The First Impression

Your image matters. According to my research, sloppiness and poor grooming are the top dating turnoffs. It is important to make yourself the most attractive person that you can be. No matter what you have to work with, you can improve your looks with regards to hair, grooming, clothes, and weight.

Here are my suggestions:

1. ***Exercise and work out several times a week.*** Use a trainer if you need discipline. Find a work-out buddy to help you stay on schedule.

   If weight is an issue for you, then find a diet or a diet program that is easy for you to stick to. You may want to consult a nutritionist to learn what diet is best for you.

   Heavy men and women succeed on the dating scene if they carry their weight well. Exercise is especially important to them because good posture can minimize figure flaws. Heavy women should emphasize their beautiful faces and dress to make the most of their shape.

2. *Get a makeover!* Hair and makeup for women, hair and grooming for men. Find your own Fab Five!

Have your wardrobe reviewed by a friend with good taste or a wardrobe consultant. Hey, guys, that goes for you too! Strive for simple elegance. Remember, a man or woman wants someone he or she feels proud to bring home to meet family and friends.

Attracting the Right Relationship by Projecting Confidence

Just as you are honest with yourself about who you are, so you must be honest with your dates about who you are. The bottom line for dating like a pro is projecting confidence as you show what's special and unique about you. This is what will attract the right people to you. You want to show that you have plenty to bring to the relationship. Here are the qualities to project on a date and in your Internet profile that will make you attractive to others—you need to use your THRIVE.

Talents and skills: What you do well. Can you mimic voices? Find just the right accessories? Are you flexible enough to do a split? Fix a computer? Bake desserts? Swim ten laps? Take great photos? Certain people will appreciate theses things about you.

Heart: Who you are inside. Do you take in strays? Visit your grandmother every week? Volunteer in a soup kitchen? Remember birthdays? The right person will bask in your light.

Reasons: You share a common goal around wanting the relationship. You both want to get married or you both just want companionship. You have the same motivation for coming together.

Interests: Your capacity for enjoyment and enthusiasm. You have your favorite spectator sports, are an avid tennis player, love country music, and are always looking for new places to travel. Or perhaps you watch World Wide Wrestling and attend Monster car rallies! Your partner will appreciate and share in some of your interests and vice versa.

Values: What is most important to you? Do you speak up for what you believe? Are you active for an environmental cause or involved in supporting children in Africa? Are you a leader in community organizations? Are you there for your family, not just your children but your parents too? Your beloved will share in your key values.

Energy: This is your *joie de vivre*, your passion and drive that shines through to others. Or perhaps you are a low-key person. Your mate will be attracted to your particular energy wavelength.

Spot Check: How Are You Doing So Far?

Answer these questions to help determine if you are *really* using the Get It Right This Time™ Method to prepare yourself for finding The Right One.

1. Do you really know your values, goals, and must-haves?

2. Have you identified your own external and internal roadblocks— the ones that might be keeping you from moving forward in a relationship?

3. Are you presenting the most attractive you?

4. Have you used T-H-R-I-V-E to identify your unique attraction qualities?

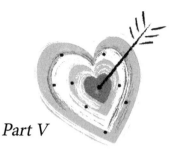

Part V

Where to Meet
The Right One

Putting yourself out there to meet other singles can seem like a lot of work. Dating people you know only from the Internet or a phone conversation may be overwhelming. Just remember: You are able to exert all this effort because you believe it's going to work—that before long you are going to meet that special someone. I'm here to tell you, yes, it does happen. Here are some of the places you are likely to find love. There are only so many hours in the day and so many options of where to look for your future partner, especially if you live in a metropolitan area. So, how do you choose which venue is The Right One for you to pursue?

How Your Values, Your Passions, Your Personality Will Guide You

What place or activity would give you the greatest chance of success to meet that someone special? In choosing the places you will go to meet your ideal partner, you need to consider three things about yourself: your values, your passions, and your personality.

Your Values

Your values give you clues about where you need to look for a serious relationship. Consider whether religious activities, community service, political causes, environmental nature excursions, etc., will attract the kind of person who shares your core values.

We hold our values close to the center of our beings. Values are what matters to us, what we believe. Each one of us has his or her own set of values, the things we treasure most. When you have to compromise a value, you can do it, but compromise will make you unhappy. That's because we all have an emotional connection to the values we have developed from our family, education, experience, and culture. Values are what you share with the people you hang out with, from your grandmother to your best friend to possibly an office mate at work. Your values can guide you to the places where you are most likely to find a mate. If you value safety and security for those who may not be able to protect themselves in our society, then you can meet people who share this value by volunteering at the shelter for teenage runaways and by getting involved with either publicizing the shelter to at-risk youth or helping with the shelter's annual fundraising race. This is true for many good causes, from saving the environment to civil rights. There are myriad ways to get involved and meet others who share your values and might be right for you as an ideal mate.

You will meet wonderful people by working for a common cause:

- Helping the victims of a natural disaster—working on a fundraiser in your area.
- Your desire to save the environment. Meet at an Earth Day rally or work with a local environmental group.
- Your belief in helping children in need. Get involved with the Children's Hospital benefit in your area or reading English to immigrant children.

Coach Amy's Dating Wisdom

Try to pick activities and singles groups that meet fairly regularly and are not just one-shot deals. If you go only once, you may never get a chance to talk to someone you saw out of the corner of your eye. Think about joining a softball team or a bowling team, or participating in a biking or hiking group that gets together regularly. Consider attending a lecture series and cooking classes. By going regularly, you can observe how someone behaves and treats people over a period of time. You get to know people beyond a superficial level. Believe it or not, familiarity can be conducive to romance!

Your Passions

Your passions guide you in choosing activities that you enjoy. Passions drive you to activities that you excel at and support, whether athletic, cultural, or spiritual.

Our passions are the supercharged values that drive us. A passion can be your crusade to beautify your condo area, a zest for skiing, or a keen interest in documentary films. The person whose passion is old architecture can follow his or her passion by giving or taking a walking tour—and maybe meet The Right One in the process. Look to your passions to meet like-minded people. Also, choose activities that you are interested in but not passionate about to meet people who are complementary to you. A client who was a marathon runner found he was not meeting the women he liked while training and racing. He felt they were too driven and too competitive. He joined the Chinese Marching and Chowder Society near his office and spent time learning to cook Chinese food with this group at outdoor sites around the city. He was not much of a cook, but he enjoyed it. He also met a woman who is a superb cook there, and today they are engaged. He chose something he was not an expert at not only to learn a new skill but also to go to an activity where it would be likely to meet women—and it paid off.

Your Personality

Your personality determines which kinds of events are right for you. Your personality tells you how long you are most likely to hang out at an event, how frequently you want to attend, and how large or small the crowd can be in order to fit your comfort range.

There are many personality types, but here are a few to give you guidelines about yourself:

The Social Butterfly doesn't stick with one person and prefers to meet as many people as possible. One of my Social Butterfly clients went on a singles weekend where she met a lovely man who met her at the beginning of the weekend and wouldn't let go. She had gone to meet people, so she told him it was nice meeting him and she would see him around. Her hope was that he would call her anyway when they got back home from the weekend. Sure enough, he found another woman instantly that weekend and ended up marrying her. My client brought me a copy of *Jewish Week* with the happy couple pictured in it. He was a keeper, but she was too much of a Social Butterfly to be comfortable pairing off so fast.

The High Brow always thinks there is something better and is reluctant to stoop to blue-collar activities like bowling or nerd-like activities such as computer clubs. High Brows may play golf instead of joining a softball team because they think it's higher class. However, once they are in an activity, they may find they enjoy it. One of my clients was invited to join the bowling league at his company. He scoffed at the prospect but did it anyway because it made him look like a good corporate citizen. He began by saying, "Why would I want to bowl? It's so blue-collar to be dating women in the bowling league." Now, he really looks forward to Wednesday nights and hanging out with the women.

The Shy Person will not feel comfortable at a big party with lots of strangers. The shy person will not want to spend a weekend with a bunch of singles she has never met before. The Internet has been a blessing to shy people around the world because with email the other person gets to know you instead of relying on superficial outward appearances. Because the Internet is set up for one-to-one interaction, it's easier to get to know someone by conversing first via email and then by phone before you meet the other person. You've already warmed up the relationship instead of meeting the person cold, as you would at a singles event.

For shy people, a structured activity like a class or a sports league makes engaging with others easier. One of my shy clients took up dancing to meet women. Although he is normally very quiet, dancing helped him feel suave, and women loved to dance with him.

Where to Go to Meet The Right One

You want to honor your personality as you go out there looking for your one-and-only. Here are some suggestions to meet people based on certain values, passions, personalities, and interests:

If you are spiritual... Let's say you value a "spiritual connection with God"; then, religious groups at churches and synagogues are good places to go to meet other people like you. Many have singles groups that meet fairly regularly. If you are spiritual and not affiliated with any particular religion, then you might consider groups that promote general spirituality, like the Unitarian Church, Bahai, and the Humanist Society.

There are many travel opportunities for spiritual people, like ashrams where you can spend a weekend, or tours of Israel and the Holy Land. The structure of organized trips gives shy people a chance to connect with others over common interests and beliefs. Even High Brows find people they like at spiritual gatherings, since the attitudes there are nonjudgmental and open. They may even find a high-class group to attend.

Stanley, in his late thirties, met Linda, who was thirty-five, at a Shabbat dinner at a Manhattan Synagogue. He went several times before he saw Linda, and it took him a couple more dinners before he got the chance to ask her out. Luckily, he persevered, and now they are married! Another client, Jennifer, was divorced with a child. She went regularly to her church on Sundays. That's where she met Steve, who was also divorced. Given their situations with their children, they took the relationship slowly and eventually got married.

If you are athletic... "Stylish, fit, healthy, and active" are among characteristics I personally value. I participated a lot in sports to meet men, and I eventually met my husband at a singles biking group.

Robert was a very active guy who biked, played softball, bowled, and hiked. He met Audrey, who also enjoyed these same activities. Over the course of a year and running into each other again and again, they eventually started dating and are now married. Barbara, who was divorced with three kids, joined the community bowling league (mostly singles and coed) and met Jeff, who had never been married. They have been a couple for more than ten years now.

If you are not athletic but still value staying active, you might join a walk for a good cause, in the hope of meeting someone who also believes in that cause. If you aren't athletic but being healthy is one of your values, you might consider taking a natural foods cooking class, which will surround you with people who also value being healthy. This would be a good place to meet your ideal mate. Social butterflies like the crowds and excitement of group athletic activities, but for the shy person there is always the pleasure of partaking in the activity instead of singles socials, where he or she would most likely be left out standing around with a lot of strangers.

If you care about animals...Let's say you are passionate about animals. This is a passion many people share. If you volunteer with the humane society, you will meet many people who are looking for a pet. It's a great place for the social butterfly. If you like the quiet excitement of bird watching, joining the Audubon Society is a chance to be around a group of similar people on a regular basis. Leslie, who attended the Smithsonian's group regularly, met her second husband, Brad, on an Audubon outing. Bird watching is an international activity, so there is the opportunity for traveling to exotic spots to watch rare species, a wonderful opportunity for the High Brow.

To find someone who loves dogs as much as you do, consider hanging out at your local dog park or going to a "doggy brunch" put on by a singles organization. For cat lovers and other pet lovers, there are always Internet sites like www.animalattraction.com.

If you are community-oriented...Let's say community service is very important to you, then by helping out at a soup kitchen or with local politics, you will find people who share this value with you. You can look into single volunteer groups that offer opportunities to meet others in major cities and through synagogues or churches. You can get involved with your local political group to support a candidate you believe in. You may share this passion with another who could be just the right person for you!

If you are adventuresome and love travel... There are many opportunities for travel with singles. Because tours last for a week or more and because cruises create an environment for networking, travel can be a wonderful way to meet your ideal mate. The shy adventurer might find a tour with an educational angle, such as visiting the museums of Florence or climbing upon a whaling ship in Nantucket, less intimidating because it has a purpose beyond just socializing. Backroads and Steppin' Out Adventures offer tours for action-minded adventurers. For the High Brow, alumni association cruises and tours sponsored by cultural organizations like opera companies or art museums offer the seal of quality.

Gary from Chicago met Brooke from New Jersey on a trip to Thailand. Although it was a small group of fifteen professional singles in their thirties, they clicked right away. "You really get to know someone when you are with them practically twenty-four hours a day for two weeks," he told me. They are now married and living in a Chicago suburb.

If you are into personal growth... You may consider lectures, workshops, and weekends that feature some aspect of personal growth. One of my clients is into metaphysics and goes to a group that has different lectures on the subject, as well as a spiritual center. He also went on the Internet to a site that attracts people who are into personal growth activities and met a woman to date. Support groups are great for meeting people in search of learning more about themselves and sharing a common bond of going through a traumatic experience. Valerie, who was going through a divorce, met her current partner at her divorce support group meetings. In addition, several couples I know have met through my life coaching school, where they share the values of self-awareness and personal growth.

If you love music... you have found one of the main ways singles connect with their ideal partners. Studies have shown that taste in music is one of the best indicators of overall compatibility. Most towns and all major cities have community choruses where you can perform every kind of music with others. Music festivals allow you to share your favorite music in a beautiful setting with others, among whom may be your one-and-only. If you play the guitar or the violin, you might want to join an ensemble or chamber group that meets regularly. Volunteering as an usher at the symphony or at a music hall series will also ensure regular exposure to people like yourself. This is a great way to meet your ideal partner. A client volunteers every summer at Tanglewood in the Berkshires. Through her activities there and her mutual friends, she met Dennis a couple years back, whom she dated for that summer.

*If you love movies...*you have a large pool of like-minded film enthusiasts to meet at film festivals, film societies, special series, and courses in film history. If you are a filmmaker yourself, you can meet others who share your interest in film courses and at film lectures. A great way for cinema lovers to get to know others is to head over to opening day for a major release. Standing in line for hours to get in gives you a chance to chat with other film buffs and maybe start the relationship of your dreams.

*If you are interested in the arts...*check out lectures, social groups, fundraisers, and discussion groups at an area museum. Many times, singles groups have events at different cultural venues around town. On Internet sites like Craig's List and Meetup.com you can find people who meet regularly to visit museums and historic sites as a group. Try going to gallery receptions at your favorite local gallery. If you go back to the same one on a regular basis, you will surely see others who have the same taste in art as you and most likely will build a rapport with them.

*If you crave intellectual stimulation...*go find a group of people who play bridge or get into strategic gaming. Perhaps attending an adult education course at your local university or a college alumni lecture and discussion will put you in an intellectually challenging environment. One of my divorced clients started going to bridge tournaments around the country. She met her fiancé, who lived in another city, through such an activity.

By being true to your values, personality, and passions, you will find yourself with people you can relate to and be comfortable around. With this approach you increase your odds of meeting that someone special, given your limited time and dollars to devote to this endeavor.

Note: For further information on where to meet singles to date, please refer to the articles and podcast audios on my website, www.HeartmindConnection.com.

Coach Amy's Dating Wisdom

No matter what your dating strategy, the Internet can jumpstart it. When clients tell me they want to date someone in the neighborhood or in their industry or from their temple, I tell them to go out on the Internet anyway. One of my clients in Bethesda met her husband, who lived in the same county, through the Internet. So your true love can be literally just down the street from you! You need to consider the Internet as one of several ways that you will look for The Right One.

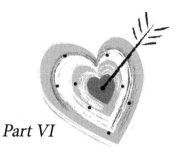

Part VI

The Dating Process

Believe it or not, there are some men and women who have not ventured into Internet dating yet. By not exploring this avenue, these people are missing an important resource for meeting wonderful men and women like themselves who are also looking to meet someone rewarding to date through more than just the traditional means and their normal daily activities.

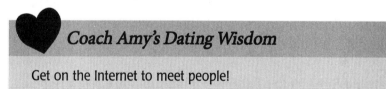

Coach Amy's Dating Wisdom

Get on the Internet to meet people!

Finding The Right One on the Internet

1. *Some people feel uncomfortable putting themselves "out there" on the Internet because it seems like sacrificing their privacy.* There is the element of personal danger if some weirdo who finds out who you are can stalk you; but there is the more likely problem that you have worked hard for a reputation at work and in your community and don't want the world to know you are looking for love online. I recommend setting up a dedicated email at one of the free services like Yahoo or Hotmail for dating. Don't use it for anything else. Once you have met the person, you can share information like your last name, your address, and your

job location. This goes for men as well as for women. Even though men are more likely to be stalkers, I have known women to be stalkers, as well. Even worse, you may find that men and women who are angry that a date did not work out as they had hoped will badmouth you.

2. ***Internet dating is definitely a numbers game.*** You can give your Internet profile more mass appeal by fudging on things like education (too much as well as too little!), expectations, and interests. You can use a glam picture from five years ago. In terms of meeting people, however, I urge you to go for quality and not quantity. The response rate is low on the major sites—less than 10%. So you have to contact a lot of people to get a connection. I had a client contact more than one hundred women. He got about a dozen responses. But in that small group, he found his girlfriend.

3. ***By opening up your geographic search, you are giving yourself a better chance of finding The Right One.*** There have been many cross-continental connections as well as connections up and down the East Coast. Of course, you have to deal with the issues of long-distance dating. Isn't it worth it for The Right One?

Getting Set Up for Internet Dating—A Checklist

Have you done your homework? Do have a clear sense of who you are—your values, life goals, and must-haves? If your answer is yes, you are now ready to go online. I received confirmation from a former client, now in a long-term relationship with a woman he met on the Internet, who told me, "What you did for me was to help me clarify what I really wanted in a partner. Without that, I'd be spinning my wheels."

It's best to present the most authentic you! *What you put out there is what you will attract.* By putting out false information, you will attract someone for false reasons. The relationship won't go anywhere. I suggest you use your THRIVE model to attract The Right One.

Your photograph is all-important. You will want to make sure the picture is attractive, warm, and inviting. Avoid the serious look with mouth turned down. I do recommend my clients invest in a professional photo. The photo needs to be recent. Otherwise, the disappointment will kill the interest as soon as you meet. Not only will your date discover you don't look like that anymore, he or she will question your ethics.

Internet Dating Strategies: Women versus Men

Many women may wait for the guy to contact them. The purpose of your online profile is to attract the right men to contact you. It's okay to wink. That may spark interest in someone who may have inadvertently overlooked you. However, how do you feel about a guy who sits back and waits for women to contact him? Or, perhaps, he has already passed you over. Regardless, how flattering it is for the guy when you make the move!

Men, you need to seek out the women who interest you. The purpose of your online profile is to pique the interest of women so they will take the time to contact you back once you have initiated contact. You want to minimize the turnoffs in your profile because those are the things that will keep women from contacting you back. You want women to say, "Hmmm—he seems interesting!"

Infinite Possibilities

Many people meet on the Internet, and quite a few of them become friends, lovers, and even spouses. There are more than three hundred dedicated dating sites serving every taste. In addition, many general sites like Craig's List have dating classifieds where you can connect with people city by city. I tell my clients that the Internet is like a huge party. You will meet every kind of person, and you want to be sure that you present yourself at your best. It's just as important to remain skeptical about the people you meet on the Net—maintain your distance and be safe until you feel the person is trustworthy.

Definitely do a Google search on your potential date to check out whether his or her information is accurate; you may even consider hiring a private detective before becoming too serious!

Getting Your Profile Online

You finally bite the bullet and decide to try Internet dating. You have narrowed down one or two sites recommended by your friends, where they have had success meeting people. Now you have to write your Internet profile. That's the hard part! Be careful not to be too influenced by others' bad Internet dating experiences. Your values, personality, and attitude may lead to a more positive outcome.

Or you have had your Internet dating profile up for a while and have not seen much action lately. Per-haps it is time for you to reevaluate your profile to see whether you can make im-provements to attract more quality candidates.

Hope she wrote back!

How do you pack-age yourself in a way that will attract the right people to you? What if writing is not your forte? If you fol-low the five ideas outlined below, you will be putting your best foot forward and on your way to experiencing the excitement of Internet dating, or revitalizing your Internet potential.

For those new to Internet dating, after checking out the format of the profile and how others are presenting themselves, I encourage you to:

1. *Tell your audience what's unique about you.* What sets you apart from the next guy or gal? What is special about you? Do you have any special talents? You want someone who appreciates that about you. If you have an artistic bent or you sing in a chorus, describe that! If you run marathons or help out with volunteer activities, put that down. This will set you apart from all the other Internet profiles out there.

2. *Take your reader into your experiences with you.* I believe in bringing the reader into the experiences that you truly value. Don't just superficially mention you like running through the park, but send out an invitation for him or her to join you. For instance, one of my clients described how he loves to jog in a city park in the fall when the air is crisp and the leaves are multitonal. Doesn't this description have a "come join me" feeling?

   Don't just mention that you like concerts and movies. Describe what kind of concerts you prefer and types of movies you love.

3. *Describe what's truly important to you.* What gets you up in the morning? What truly motivates you in life? One of my clients truly values giving of herself to the community. She is an avid volunteer. I'm sure she wants to attract someone who also values giving to the community as well. When you get beyond the superficial, you will attract those who say, "This person seems to be the kind of person I want to meet!"

4. *Invest in hiring a professional for the all-important photo.* We do live in a visual society, and we do judge a book by its cover! Studies have shown that the photo is the key to whether a person decides to check out your profile or not. If you are not sure how you come across in the photo, then ask friends or co-workers for their opinions. I request my clients to get a professional photo 95% of the time. And make sure the photo is a current one of you, within a year or two!

Some Internet dating sites do provide you with a list of photographers in your area who specialize in Internet dating photos. As an added bonus, you will have a photo of yourself to give to your family members for the holidays come December.

Internet Dating Do's and Don'ts

About Your Picture on the Site

- Do look friendly and approachable.
- Do put the best picture possible on your profile.
- Don't put just any mug shot of you on your site.
- Don't be with other people. Dog, cat, and kids are okay!

About Your Profile on the Site

- Do include what's unique about you and why someone will want to go out with you.
- Do describe your values in the body of the profile. What's fulfilling for you? What do you treasure?
- Do try to be as descriptive as possible so the reader will experience what you do. Help them see, smell, and hear the beach. Put in a "come play with me" quality!
- Do consider widening your search to include more possible potential partners.
- Don't put stuff in your profile that isn't putting your best foot forward.
- Don't lie! Be honest and upbeat. That doesn't mean you have to reveal all your faults!

About Contacting Each Other

- Do go after quality and not just quantity!
- Do find something that you connect to. A cause, a passion, or an interest can be an excellent basis for a relationship.
- Do email back and forth a couple of times to get a sense of the person: their way of thinking and how they express themselves.
- Don't be a pen pal forever! If the person is unwilling to talk on the phone, stop the interchange. Do talk on the phone to gain further rapport.
- Do trust your intuition. If something doesn't feel right, don't pursue it any further. Listen to your internal red flags.
- Don't talk on the phone for weeks without making plans to get together.

Ready to Meet

- Do give each other cell phone numbers in case something happens on your way to the meeting. (I once had a fender bender driving to meet a date.)
- Do meet in a public place for coffee during the day.
- Don't run away if the person doesn't look like what you thought he or she would look like.
- Don't give out too much information about yourself before you know the person better.
- Don't expect the other person to pay. Be prepared to pay your share. It will be a nice surprise if the other person picks up the check.
- Do give a date the benefit of the doubt and agree to meet again if there is any interest at all. Chemistry can develop over time.
- Don't expect an "instant" relationship just because you have been corresponding on the Internet for weeks.
- Do beware of becoming too physical too fast. You may be overstepping the other person's boundaries by getting physical right away.
- Do respect the need for your date to pace the relationship in order for him or her to feel comfortable with you. Some people are shy.

Following Up

- Do be honest about your level of interest in the person. Consider that you may want to keep him or her as a friend or sports partner or on your party list. Also, the person may know someone else you'd like to meet.
- Do thank the person for a nice time. If your date paid, be sure to thank him or her and not let it seem like a given.
- Don't say you'll call and not call!
- Don't wait a month to call if you liked your date. Your date may have moved onto the next prospect.

Face-to-Face Dating Tips

Let's say during the last couple of weeks you have communicated with someone of interest via email and several telephone conversations. There is obvious "phone chemistry" and mutual interest in meeting each other. You both agree to meet in person—now for the moment of truth!

This step-by-step dating guide will help you not miss a beat in the dating dance. Remember: You not only get to choose your partner but you also get to choose your dance.

A Successful First Date—Especially If You Have Never Met the Person Before!

1. **Visualize success.** Think about your wonderful attributes and not your faults. Take an inventory of your values, skills, talents, interests, and "heart." Leave all your negative thoughts at home.

2. **Keep your expectations in check.** Don't start imagining yourself at the altar with your date. Ask yourself these three questions: Do I like the person? Does the conversation flow easily? Is there any kind of attraction? That's it. If you answer yes to these questions, then be open to seeing the person again.

3. **Dress appropriately for a date.** Be presentable, neat, well-groomed, and in casual dress clothes. Men, don't come in a T-shirt and jeans, and women, do not come dressed to kill by looking overly sexy like you are going to a nightclub. Strive to look like the guy or girl next door and someone it would be proper to bring home to your date's parents.

4. **Be prepared to discuss at least five general topics.** Prepare a list of topics, like current events and subjects of personal interest to you, such as your work, volunteer activities, hobbies, favorite travel destinations, any books you are reading, any movies you have seen lately, and favorite sports to watch or participate in. Do not talk about your divorce or your last boyfriend. If you

have children, you may talk about them briefly—do not bore your date with hours of stories about your kids.

5. *Use your values as your guideposts.* Know what's most important to you and look to see if your date has similar feelings. Pay close attention to anything that makes you uncomfortable—your gut is usually right!

6. *Pick a quiet place where you can talk.* Meeting at a coffee house or a bookstore is best. You may decide to take a stroll if it feels right. Don't get involved in a meal since paying for the meal may become an issue. Also, don't go to a show or a movie where it's difficult to talk.

7. *Plan on spending one to two hours max.* The purpose of your first encounter is to see the person and to get a feel for him or her. It's best not to drag the date on. Besides, you need to leave some stuff to talk about during subsequent dates!

8. *It is best to meet during the day.* It is more relaxed to meet in the late morning or afternoon during the weekend. A weekday evening is the next best thing. Weekend evenings are too much pressure and feel like a serious date. You may be tempted to do stuff you will later regret!

9. *Always be courteous and kind to your date—even if you are not interested.* You never know where you will see him or her again and who his or her friends are. Always treat people the way you wish to be treated.

10. *If all goes well.* Women—be open to going out again. Studies have shown that women have gotten married to men they were not really interested in at first. Men—trust your gut. If you are not attracted, be pleasant and be honest. Never say, "I'll call" and not call!

By following the above tips, you will most likely have a more pleasant first date experience. It may well lead to future dates if you so desire!

People Date People They Trust

That's a fact! What actions and behaviors encourage you to trust someone? Trust is earned through many positive interactions and over time. Some behaviors that reinforce trust are:

- Telling the whole truth even if it's about sex, money, health problems.
- Staying sincere: no placating just to keep the peace.
- Being reliable: calling when you say you will call.
- Sharing emotions: not being afraid to speak up if you are scared or angry.
- Remaining rational: no ranting, yelling, or screaming obscenities.
- Maintaining self-control: no hitting or shoving no matter how angry you are.
- Keeping promises: If you say you will walk the dog, walk the dog.
- Focusing on the other person: It's not always about you!

Trust is the foundation of all relationships. And trust starts with respect. Your partner is a person with needs and wants, just as you are. Misleading your partner with half-truths or empty promises is only a winning strategy for the short term. Since people who are ready for The Right One desire to build relationships, trust is essential.

Because they want the relationship to work so much, people who are dating may be tempted to lie about important issues like finances, fidelity, and family problems. These are the very areas that are most important in building a relationship. So if you think the facts of your life might be a turnoff, build up to sharing them only after trust has been established in other areas. But don't wait too long to discuss important matters since full disclosure is a requirement for a solid future. Take a chance that your partner cares enough about you and the relationship to work out problems together and to find viable solutions.

How to Date Like an Entrepreneur

Entrepreneurs, who have to look at situations strategically if they are to thrive, have techniques that will help you in your dating. I was single while I ran a women's clothing boutique. Although I worked incredible hours and had a seven-day-a-week operation, I made a concerted effort to date and meet people, which eventually led me to meeting my husband. Here is my entrepreneur's advice.

1. *Get clear on what your life goals and priorities are.* What are your goals and priorities in life?
   - Work
   - Family
   - Finding a life partner and getting married
   - Community service
   - Athletic activities
   - Personal and/or social activities

   Rank them from 1 to 6, 1 being the most important. What do you now notice about your priorities?

   Next, where do you see yourself in five years? Would you be happy being single at that time? It's time to be honest with yourself.

   Just like you have a plan for your business, you need to develop a plan for your life. When you focus on obtaining and having the important things in life, they will happen for you.

2. *Put your personal time on your calendar and stick to it!* When you decide to carve out some time for your personal life, which may include the pursuit of meeting someone for a relationship, then make an appointment with yourself on your calendar. How many hours a week are you willing to commit to this endeavor?

You need to apply the same time-management skills to your personal time as you do to your work time. Do you consider meeting people to date to be an urgent priority, merely desirable, or something for down the road?

Go ahead, put this date in your calendar and commit to keeping this appointment with yourself!

3. *Decide on what trade-offs you are willing to make.* The entrepreneur knows life is about trade-offs. What are you willing to sacrifice to have what you want? It may be for a short time or a long time, depending on your success in meeting the right person for you.

Like an entrepreneur, you must be willing to work fewer hours and make less money. Perhaps you would be willing to hire someone to help you with routine tasks. I hired a bookkeeper even though I was very capable of doing the work myself. I ended up using a mailing service for my promotional materials whereas, early on in my business, I had done the mailing labels myself. Consider hiring an assistant to help you with writing letters, making appointments, and following up with phone calls to your clients.

4. *Use efficient dating techniques.* There is a time cost and benefit to every singles event and dating service available to you. Once you have a handle on how much time a week you want to devote to dating, then you need to decide how much money you want to devote to these endeavors.

The best thing you can do for yourself is to get a really clear picture of your values. Your values are what are most important to you in life. For instance, kindness and compassion may be very important to you. Therefore, this is what you would want in a mate as well. Once you have your values constructed, you have guideposts for which you can evaluate your potential partner.

Many entrepreneurs go for Internet dating because they can do it on the road, at odd hours, and on their own terms. You can search the Net at all hours of the day or night. As an enterprising businessperson would do, try more than one site. Different sites will produce different results. See my resource page at www.HeartmindConnection.com for suggestions.

Lastly, ask friends, family, or perhaps business associates who know you well to introduce you to people to date. Tell them what you are looking for in a mate, so they can be helpful to you. Don't be shy to ask them to fix you up. One of my clients was very good about getting the word out at networking events that she was looking to meet someone to date. She eventually got fixed up with someone she really likes.

5. **_Combine fun and recreation with meeting people._** What is fun and relaxing for you? It is not healthy to work all the time and not have any play!

If you enjoy socializing, then the singles events may help you get out and be with people. Who knows, you may pick up a client if not a date! For athletic types, sports activities such as biking groups or tennis parties may be a way to have fun and meet someone to date. If you are into working out to keep your shape and stamina, then the gym can be a place to meet like-minded members of the opposite sex. Perhaps you will entertain taking a ski trip or a hiking trip with a singles group.

Taking vacations is critical to maintaining sanity for an entrepreneur. If you love traveling, you may consider joining a singles travel group. There are even singles cruises, which give you plenty of leisure time for socializing and meeting new people on the ship. I know a woman who loved yoga and found a travel group that incorporated daily yoga into the trip. Imagine finding your soul mate while doing what you truly love!

As an entrepreneur in the dating world, you have a vision of what you want, and focus on that goal. If you apply drive and determination to dating, you will see results.

Checklist for the Dating Process

It's great when a date turns out to be a wonderful person, but as you get to know one another better, there are issues that can and probably will come up. Since you are dating with a purpose—to establish a lasting relationship—you don't want to waste time, your own or your date's—on a relationship that is going nowhere. Here are some guidelines for knowing when it is time to leave a relationship and move on.

1. *If you are not getting what you need.* If you feel needy and there is something missing, then that's a sign something is not working for you. Can you put your finger on it?

   One of my clients wished the man she was dating would drop her an email or a phone call during the week, just to show that he was thinking of her. She suggested this to him, but he didn't contact her beyond setting up their dates for the weekend. She decided to stop dating him because his focus on his work life would never allow him to spend time connecting with her during the week. She felt that staying in touch should come naturally to him and would demonstrate to her that the relationship was progressing forward. Since he never was able to give her what she needed, she wasn't able to feel connected to him, and they stopped dating.

2. *Personal boundaries have been ignored.* Here are some examples of some personal boundaries that may get overstepped:
   - He gets too physical too early.
   - She wants to get involved with your kids right away.
   - He wants to see you every day!

   Pay attention if something feels uncomfortable to you. Try to get a sense of your personal boundaries and stick to them!

3. *Your life goals are different:*
   - You want marriage, and he doesn't.
   - He wants a family, and you don't.

- She is open to adoption, and he isn't.
- You live in different cities, and neither is willing to move.

4. *There is a non-negotiable or must-have that you can't live with:*
   - He wants a tidy house, and you are comfortable with clutter.
   - She drinks quite a lot, and you don't drink at all.
   - He wants to spend weekends in the city, and you want to spend weekends at the beach.

5. *Your key relationship values are not aligned.* You value kindness and generosity, and you find your date is stingy and cheap. Or, you value discretion, and your partner can't keep a secret. You await occasions for sharing difficult confidences whereas your partner likes to know when things are wrong as soon as they happen.

   These may seem trivial, but it is critical that you share your core values with your life partner.

6. *Respect has been lost or never was there.* Here are some examples of disrespectful behavior:
   - S/he criticizes you.
   - S/he screams obscenities at you.
   - A woman harps on a man because he is not working. One client had an issue with a boyfriend who didn't have any retirement savings; down deep, she felt he was irresponsible. Although he was a very nice person, this relationship did not last because she did not respect him, and they didn't share this value around money.
   - Think about what doesn't feel right to you in the relationship. Love may not be expressed in a way that you need. For example, you enjoy public displays of affection, and the guy just doesn't do PDA!
   - He wants to spend all his free time with you, and you enjoy spending time with your friends as well.
   - S/he really doesn't want to hang out with your kids.

Be willing to express what you need and want from the other person. You may be afraid to ask for what you need in a relationship. You leave the relationship to avoid a confrontation with your partner. That doesn't give your date a chance to step up to the plate and honor your request.

Make Some Decisions on How Long It Is Acceptable for You...

- To date someone before expecting to be exclusive
- To consider living together or not
- To be in a relationship exclusively before expecting a more serious commitment or engagement

If you know what to look for in others and are clear about what you want for yourself, dating becomes less of an emotional roller coaster. By focusing on your goal of the right romantic relationship, you can tolerate rejection from daters who have different goals from your own. You will also learn from the experience not to go through the agony of taking rejection personally.

Dating depends on timing. You may be thirty-two and eager to find The Right One, but not everyone in your age group is ready to settle down. Being rejected by someone your age because she is still dating to have fun is not a rejection of you; it is simply that the timing is off.

Part VII

Is This The Right One?

Coach Amy's Dating Wisdom

As a couple, you need to figure out what works for you in such a way that each person satisfies his or her particular needs. Don't use anyone else's standards. So if someone says, "How can you let your husband go out without you?" you can say, "My husband loves to be with people—I have too much to do at home (or with my work) and I am too tired when I get home from work—besides, I trust him!"

People utilizing the Get It Right This Time™ Method know the feeling of "This is it!" followed by the disappointment when the relationship fizzles out. Don't let this happen to you. Once you have met someone special, make a conscious effort to keep your partner happy with the Triple A: appreciation, affection, and attention.

Qualities of The Right One

All of the stress of dating seems worth it when you meet someone special. The world feels like a brighter place, and you look forward to the future rather than dread it. When you meet a person who makes you happy, step back for a few minutes and check out his or her qualities. As human beings, we all respond to certain behaviors positively. Here are the qualities in a partner with whom you can have long-term bliss:

1. *An attentive ear.* You want someone who can be your best friend through thick and thin, who can share your deepest thoughts and hear what you are saying, whether the situation is serious or fun.

2. *A compassionate heart.* Does he take in stray animals? Does she volunteer to help the sick? And how forgiving is his or her nature? Does this person empathize with you when you've had a bad day?

3. *A supportive spirit.* You hope your partner is your greatest fan. He cheers you on during difficult times at the office. She supports you by taking care of the kids at night while you go back to school. You share each other's tensions and triumphs.

4. *A special understanding.* Every human strives for acceptance. Showing you that you are seen and known is the biggest gift a partner can give. Does your partner pay attention to you? Does he or she affirm your special way of doing things?

5. *A sense of appreciation.* The ability to recognize when you have gone out of your way or done something nice is a lost art. Just saying these simple words, "I appreciate what you have done," can make your day. Does your partner value your efforts? Even if it's doing the laundry?

6. *A willing intimacy.* In a relationship, you make yourself vulnerable to another person. Being willing to show your true self to another does take guts and trust. It is not an everyday occurrence. Does your partner share with you the good and the bad to feel closer to you?

7. *An abiding respect.* Remaining respectful in times of disagreement or stress takes a lot of class. A harsh word can break your strong bond with the slip of a hurtful tongue. Is your partner taking your feelings into consideration when he or she speaks?

8. *A commitment to making the relationship work.* As part of a couple, partners need to be willing to listen to constructive comments and reasonable requests. Is your partner willing to talk things out? Is he or she willing to get third-party help (like counseling) when you reach an impasse?

9. *An enduring trust.* Trust is built over time and many positive encounters with someone. Does your partner follow up when he or she makes a promise? Is this someone you have found you can count on? Trust is the foundation of any relationship.

10. *Pride in being part of a couple.* Does your potential partner think of how his or her actions will affect you? Can he or she compromise for the sake of the relationship? A relationship cannot survive on "me" alone!

These are the ten qualities you want in the mate you choose. You also want to develop these qualities in yourself so you can be a loving partner. Only you know which of these qualities are most important to you. Once you have found them in a person, cherish them. Remember that your partner is appreciating these qualities in you as well. With these attitudes and attributes, you can build a lasting relationship.

Taking That Leap of Faith into Commitment

Putting yourself out there to meet The Right One is a lot of work. Dating people you know only from the Internet or a phone conversation can seem overwhelming. Just remember: You are able to exert all this effort because you believe it's going to work—that before long you are going to meet that special someone. I'm here to tell you, yes, it does happen. But how can you tell when it is happening to you? What are the signs that he or she is The Right One?

There are signs that a relationship has lasting value. There is more to it than simply "being in love." You are committing yourself to a lifelong relationship, so you will want to think about where you will be in ten years, in twenty, in fifty. Think about how you feel about your partner now and imagine how you might feel when you are taking the grandchildren to Disney World thirty years from now. Ask yourself four questions about the relationship you are now in:

1. Chemistry—Do I get a lift just seeing this person?

2. Love—Do I want to help this person be comfortable and confident so that he or she can follow his or her dreams?

3. Common Goals—Do I share dreams for ten years from now with this person?

4. Shared Values—Do our priorities mesh? Do we care about the same things?

In my interviewing I have found that these are the criteria that couples most often cite as reasons for why they took the leap of faith into a committed relationship.

The couples I coach sometimes express surprise at how much work it takes to keep a good relationship going. Yes, it does take work, but you will both agree that keeping the communication open and the love flowing pays back a thousandfold.

Six Signs You Have Found The Right One

1. *There is a feeling of "home."* There is a sense of comfort. The person you are dating feels so naturally right that it seems preordained. You just know this person is The One. It's like you have known each other your whole life because it's so easy to talk to one another. You feel familiarity with your partner. You can be sitting on the beach with nothing else going on, and just being together is enough.

2. *There is a flow.* The relationship has ease. Time just flies when you are with the right person. Yes, relationships take work, but this is joyous work. The concept of flow is true for both in and out of the bedroom! For instance, at dinner in a cute Italian res-

taurant, instead of ordering two entrees, you order two appetizers and one entrée to share your choices. You have a spirited discussion about which wine to order. He wins, but you are pleasantly surprised that you adore his choice. Without a big effort, things just move along.

3. **You are able to laugh together, have fun, and enjoy each other's company.** You enjoy each other's sense of humor even though you may not have exactly the same humor, and you do crack a smile. On our second date, my husband and I were sitting in a restaurant booth, and both of us blew straw wrappings at each other—like kids! We both had a good laugh. It's okay to be silly with the right person.

4. **You are each other's best friend.** There is a sense of trust and loyalty. You know your partner will be there for you through thick and thin. Your partner can be counted on to give you the benefit of the doubt when others find fault with you. You want to share everything with this person—the good stuff *and* the bad stuff. If the boss doesn't appreciate her work, you are the one who encourages her to apply for a transfer and assures her that others will see her strengths—just as you do.

5. **You are passionately fond of one another.** You arrive from the airport after midnight, exhausted. He has been waiting up and leaps to the door and throws his arms around you. You know he's genuinely happy you're back. It's not an act. He really wants to be right next to you because he's missed you so much the past three days.

6. **You both act in a "we" way rather than a "me" way.** She loves scuba diving, and you love hiking. Instead of heading for either the Caribbean for her or the Appalachian Trail for you, you research options until you find that resort in Costa Rica where she can dive and you can hike. Even better, the resort has golf facilities that you can enjoy together. Whether for long-term or

short-term goals, you make decisions that benefit the relationship instead of only the individual. You share life goals and work toward them together. You care about how your actions affect the other person. You are willing to work out your differences to keep your partnership going.

Part VIII

The Dream Comes True

You cannot assume that it will last if you and your partner don't make an effort. There are many ways to keep the flame going in a relationship for the long term to show caring and keep communications open.

How Do You Express Love?

Let me tell you about one of my clients. During our phone coaching sessions we were discussing the upcoming anniversary of when he met his girlfriend. He really wanted to make it a special occasion and arranged to take her out for dinner to a very fancy restaurant. He told me he also planned to bring her flowers.

I told him that flowers were a beautiful gift, but flowers die. What women love is jewelry! "When you buy jewelry, you're buying something she can wear to remind her of you and to show off to her friends," I told him. "Just imagine her saying, 'This is what my boyfriend bought me. Don't you love it?'" I also told him that it needn't be expensive. "You can buy her a beautiful sterling silver bracelet or a nice necklace that looks very substantial for a very reasonable price."

He took my advice and bought her a beautiful sterling silver and onyx necklace and earrings set. He came to our next call and said, "I owe you big! She loved the jewelry I gave her." He felt like a hero, and I could hear him beaming on the phone! Clearly, he hit the mark with his expression of love to his girlfriend.

This is just one illustration of how people can express love to one another. Many women are shy in giving jewelry, but when a social worker client of mine gave her boyfriend, a professional guitarist, sterling cuff links to wear to his performance, he was touched and showed them off to everyone. Thoughtful acts, like picking her up unannounced at the airport after a grueling business trip or arranging a birthday party for him, can also show how much you care for your partner.

What makes you feel special and loved by someone close to you? And how do you express love to the people you care about?

Here are six expressions of love that help people feel like they matter to you:

1. **Validations and compliments.** This is expressing what you like about a person or what you admire most. Don't just think, "Wow, I really like her outfit." It's no use keeping it to yourself; you need to tell that person what you are thinking. When you compliment someone sincerely, you can make that person's day.

2. **Time together.** Some couples spend lots of time together. They spend their free time together, and they may even work together. Others may only spend time together on weekends. Whatever works is "right," but you have to ensure you are making enough time for the one you love.

3. **Helpful gestures.** Do you like it when others do stuff for you? Perhaps your girlfriend cooks you your favorite meal. How about your boyfriend getting your car washed or taken to the dealership for a tune-up? Perhaps s/he helps you buy a new computer or shop for the right home accessories.

   Here are some other examples of helpful gestures:
   - A client waits for the cable guy to fix her computer while his girlfriend's at work.
   - Another client clips articles that she thinks may be of interest to her partner.

- Another client, when his girlfriend bowed out of a date because she had a terrible cold, picked up some chicken soup at the Chinese takeout to bring to her.

4. *Tokens of affection.* Do you like to receive gifts? Is that important for you to feel loved? In my introduction—the necklace and earrings set was an example of a token of affection. If you bring a bone or a chew toy for a boyfriend's dog, that's a token of affection for both the pet and the man! I am appreciative when my husband brings home flowers for no significant reason.

I like to bring my husband a new shirt as a token of affection. Okay, I may be tired of seeing him wearing the same old thing!

5. *Physical connection.* This is the need to have affection, such as physical touch, with another in order to feel loved. This is a very basic need for some people whereas others do not like any kind of public display.

Let me tell you a story about one of my clients. He griped to me about how his girlfriend insisted on public displays of affection, such as giving him a hello kiss or holding hands. He gave me the example of his girlfriend kissing him when she met him in a restaurant. When I asked him why he was so uncomfortable with a quick kiss in a restaurant, he said he worried about what the wait staff would think. I explained to him that his girlfriend's displays of affection are normal but because of his uptightness about public displays, he should probably look elsewhere. Clearly, he and his girlfriend had different comfort levels on this matter!

Physical expressions of love mean a lot to some people. If you like a person who is uncomfortable with casual kisses and handholding, then you need to discuss with your partner your different comfort levels and how the two of you can get each other's needs met. This shows you value your partner's likes and desires and you want to find an acceptable, comfortable compromise.

6. *Being there for the tough times.* Having your close friends or significant other being there for you in bad times as well as good

may be a deal breaker for you in a relationship. Will he or she visit you in the hospital if you are sick or had a horrible accident? Will your steady boyfriend support you emotionally and perhaps financially if you are laid off? Are you understanding when someone is busy and can't be there for you, or would you just write that person off?

My husband and I had been dating for three months when he became my lifeline on September 11th, 2001. I was in New York, and he was in Washington, D.C., where I lived with my cat. He helped me find a friend to take care of my cat since I could not get home that evening. I couldn't get through to Amtrack, and Alan helped me learn if the trains were running or not. He was there to pick me up at the train station when I returned to D.C. since I was planning on flying home and my car was at the airport. It was then I knew I could count on him!

How Do Displays of Caring Help a Relationship Grow?

When love is expressed in the manner people expect and need, they will feel something special in the relationship. They will seek out the company of the person who makes them feel they are needed and wanted. Wanting to be with a person even when you are at work or traveling is the sign that they are special.

When you choose a mate, you want to find someone who can make you want to be around them more. Flattery, helpfulness, generosity, and appreciation are powerful tools in a love relationship. Some Romeos have figured this out and use these gestures to mislead women they are not seriously interested in. So you see, this stuff can be great or it can be dangerous, too!

So you may need one expression of love above all or a combination of several types of expression to feel truly loved. It's important to be honest with your partner and not be afraid to ask for what you need to feel loved!

My husband and I sat down and each wrote ten things that make us feel loved. Then we exchanged our lists. That way, we've learned each other's expectations and do not make assumptions. We both were open to each other's suggestions for ways to enhance our relationship.

Understanding and discussing the expressions of love that resonate most with you and your partner will strengthen your bond. You will feel truly loved. It's the best feeling in the world!

Having the Necessary Communication Tools to Ensure Lasting Bliss

Here are some techniques for keeping a relationship on track and going in the right direction! Electricians have the tools to mend the wiring and hang the new chandelier. Seamstresses have the tools to hide stitches and can utilize them to make a hem float. With the right tools, artisans can fix things and make great new things. In the same vein, couples need the right tools to keep communication open, healthy, and on the right track.

Fine tune your listening skills. As humans, we all want to feel heard. Focus your attention on your partner. Hear what he or she says. Try to keep your own agenda and voice out of it. Repeat back what you think you heard your partner express and ask: Did I understand you correctly? You don't have to agree with what your partner says, just show you understand his or her point of view.

Speak from "I" statements. When you say, "You always throw the dishes in the sink and never clean up by putting them in the dishwasher," you are casting blame and putting your partner on the defensive. Instead, speak from your own experience. For instance, "I am tired of always putting the dishes away into the dishwasher. I would appreciate your help in this area."

Your partner can't dispute that you are tired. You are also asking for his or her help, which is hard to turn down!

Don't assume. Turn up your curiosity volume, so you can hear what the other person is saying. Take the time to ask questions so you don't make assumptions and draw the wrong conclusion. Your partner will appreciate your trying to understand the situation better. "What" and "how" questions are better than "why" questions, which may put people on the defensive.

Come right out and ask. Many people are afraid to ask for what they want, so they complain, complain, complain. Make requests instead of complaining! What you get when you ask comes out of the way you ask for what you need. For instance, appeal to his expertise: "I really need your help on this project because I don't know as much as you do." Asking in a manner that doesn't put him down but appeals to his expertise will get you the help you need.

"Why are these projects so hard? What morons design them anyway!" is a complaint and not likely to propel your partner to want to help you.

Brainstorm solutions together. Two heads are better than one. What two can easily do is often hard for one. If she wants to attend her uncle's birthday party and he wants to catch the game, lay out the times and places. Figure out how she can be where she wants to be and he can be where he wants to be. Together, seek to find solutions that work for both of you. Put all the possible solutions on the table. Now, look at each one in terms of the pros and the cons. Most of the time, you can compromise and find a solution to the issue that will make you both happy.

Keep your word. With every commitment given and every promise made, we are building our trust in that special person. Trust, like a bank account, grows over time. When you live up to your promises, the trust bond of your relationship is reinforced.

If you add these communications tools to your toolkit, you will be working toward constructive solutions and ultimately be happier with the important people in your life!

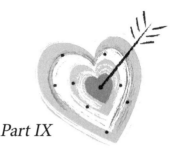

Part IX

Should You Stay in This Relationship?

At a certain point in an ongoing relationship, the subject of commitment will be raised by either your partner or you. You know what you want for yourself. If you are going to reach that goal, you have to talk about it. You want to be able to talk about anything and everything with the person you love. Once you are settled in with your partner, you will need to be able to discuss all issues, great and small. Being afraid of your partner's reaction means that you are not yet feeling secure enough in that relationship. Build up an inventory of good experiences together so that you have the courage to talk about the big issues.

The sooner you know how interested your partner is in commitment, the better off you are. If the question scares your partner, let him or her run, and watch out for smooth operators who tell you what you want to hear and string you along.

The End of the Affair

It can happen after three dates or thirty years—you start to lose that loving feeling or you never had it to begin with. It's unfortunate that many people stay in unsatisfying relationships for way too long and let life pass them by. Don't let this happen to you. Remember, the most important factor in finding The Right One is to recognize when it's not working for you and move on. If you are in a relationship, look at it honestly. Do you see any of these signs?

Warning Signs That Your Relationship Is On the Rocks

- Loss of sexual interest.
- Big increase in alcohol, sleeping pill, or tranquilizer consumption.
- Sudden interest in a sport that involves attractive members of the opposite sex.
- Longer and longer hours at work.
- Loss of interest in your career.
- Scorn for the progress you are making on your diet, your new business, or your achievements.
- Withholding information about the job, the house, the finances, the kids.
- Spending too much time arguing with the ex.
- Arrogance when your partner is with your friends and family.
- Crude remarks or insensitivity about your appearance or achievements.
- Not covering up a sneeze, burping in public, leaving the toilet seat up, and other disgusting habits that s/he used to be fastidious about.
- Making plans without consulting you.
- Answering your questions vaguely or claiming not to remember what you said.
- Shuns his or her share of the routine household chores like taking in the car or emptying the dishwasher.
- Irresponsible spending—such as making big purchases that are beyond your partner's means.
- Lack of consideration for your time.

- Waits until the very last minute to finalize plans.
- Comes home late with no good reason and no apologies.
- Forgets to call when he or she has promised.
- Keeps you waiting over an hour when you made plans to meet with no explanation.
- Over-scheduling and making no time for you.
- Lack of follow-through on when s/he said s/he would do it.
- Seems critical of you and gets defensive when you inquire about "what's wrong?"

When to Stay and When to Go

Bottom line: Are your relationship needs being met by your partner? Do you feel loved? If you feel needy, something's missing. Ask yourself: Have you been settling? If you are, what are the nonmonetary costs to you of settling?

To have a relationship work, both partners need to want the same things at the same time.

How Your Age and Life Goals Affect Your Relationship Choices

The biggest mistake I see is people keeping themselves in exclusive relationships with no definite future. Many people drift through life. They wake up at forty unmarried and wonder how it happened. I can tell you how it happened: They were not paying attention to a time frame. Do you have a specific time frame in the back of your mind when you are dating? This is especially relevant if marriage and children are your goals.

It's hard to stick with a schedule when you are in love, but it can be done. Here's how I did it, when I found myself in my late thirties with marriage and a family as my dating goal, and wanting to find The Right One.

Months 1–3	Establish exclusive relationship. Engage in sex only when your partner has committed to future-oriented exclusivity.
Months 2–5	Talk about the future and work toward a lasting commitment.
Month 6	Become seriously committed or engaged, or break up.

To make this method work, I needed to communicate my expectations within the first month. I had plenty of friends, and I didn't want to date a friend. I didn't want to get into a romantic and sexual relationship with someone who had no intention of sticking around. I had to be bold and express my dating intentions up front.

I had a client who was a divorced woman with children. She was exclusively dating a man for over a year who also was divorced with a teenager. She was ready to get married, and that was her goal. She wanted him to move into her house. Because her boyfriend hesitated and he seemed unsure about taking this step, she broke up with him. She eventually did meet a man who was on the same page, and they got married.

You will have to keep your focus, too. It's hard to ask for what you want. At the same time, you need to stay cool and relaxed. This is where it's good to be able to visualize the right person feeling the same way you do.

Be careful not to get stuck in an "almost" relationship. They are almost right but not quite. These relationships are dangerous because they can fritter away years before you decide that this person is not good for you for the long haul. Pay close attention to what doesn't mesh for you in your relationship.

How to Know When to Leave a Relationship

1. The relationship drains all your energy.
2. You have more bad times than good. You should expect one bad experience for every five good ones in a healthy relationship.
3. Your unconditional needs are not met. You feel "needy."
4. You don't feel loved and appreciated.
5. You make requests of your partner, and he or she ignores them.
6. The answer to the question "Why are we together?" is "I don't want to be alone." This answer is based on fear of being alone, not on the pleasure of having your partner in your life.
7. When you think about the person and can't remember why you are together!

Of course, no relationship is perfect. They all take some work and compromise. If you feel like you need something from the relationship, then I encourage you to discuss it with your partner. How he or she listens and responds back to you will demonstrate whether the two of you can work together in support of each other's happiness. It's important not to compromise on what is most important to you. If you can't satisfy each other's needs and desires, then it is probably time to move on!

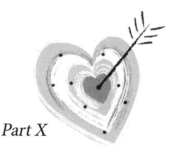

Part X

Time Frames

What Is the Right Time to Settle in with The Right One?

Until the 1970s, most American men and women did not live together as sexual partners outside of marriage. Because men had to be established financially and women had to be ready for childbearing, husbands were usually several years older than their wives.

Today, both partners make financial contributions to the relationship. On average, American men and women marry for the first time at about the same age, in their mid-twenties.

When my clients ask me "What is the best age for settling into a committed relationship?" my answer is *"Any age!"* Gloria Steinem married for the first time at 68, and Tony Randall was married for the first time at 76. Rudy Giuliani was married at 24, again at 40, and a third time at 59. My own husband and I were married when he was 48, and it was his first time! To find The Right One, you have all the time in the world or you can make it happen tomorrow. Let's look at the possibilities of settling down with The Right One.

What's the Rush?

Many people in their twenties believe that, when they have found The Right One, they have to drop everything to make room for the relationship. Sometimes these young adults are influenced by their parents' experiences of mating from the 1970s and 1980s—a totally different dating scene from the one today. For instance, a college-age client came to me last month in a panic to find a relationship. When I asked her why she was in such a hurry, she said her mother told her that if she didn't nab a guy soon, there would be younger women to replace her.

Whether they are on the rebound or just plain lonely, people in their twenties succumb to the temptation to settle into the relationship as soon as possible. So, in America, in 2006, the average age of an American at the first marriage was twenty-six. Given the poor chances of lasting marriages between people under thirty—it's not such a good idea!

After I was divorced from my first husband (whom I married at twenty-five), my father, the divorce attorney, had a little talk with me. "People should not get married until they are thirty because they do not know what they want until they are thirty!" Now I see that is wise advice. I wish I had heard it earlier and followed it!

In the twenty-first century, life is complicated and takes a lot of preparation, including education, financial stability, and emotional maturity. People in their twenties, men and women, are still developing as individuals. Their time frame for marriage should be much longer than that of older couples. Instead of rushing to the altar, couples under thirty should still be exploring what they want from a relationship. Statistics show that hooking up at an early age has a fifty-fifty chance of falling apart—so don't feel bad if you were in the half that didn't last as a couple.

I coached a beautiful young literary agent who fell in love with the first man she met out of college, a music critic. They lived together for a year, and though they were still in love, they split up, living apart and dating other people. Each wanted to have a life of his or her own. The timing just wasn't right for them.

Many relationships falter when the dreams differ. It can be heartbreaking to leave a lover because you want to go to law school and

he wants to start a family. That hard choice only pays off later when you are settled into a new relationship without feeling that you compromised your own dreams for love. That's when you will see that it was worth it to wait.

For more information on this subject, check out my e-book, *Thirty (Very Good) Reasons Not to Marry Until You Are Thirty*, available for download from my website, www.Heartmind Connection.com.

"It's Too Late for Me! I'm Over the Hill"

Many of my clients—too many—are reluctant to get out there after their relationship has failed because they feel it's too late. Whether they are twenty-seven or seventy-two, they feel like damaged goods. They are hyper-aware that they are older and not as good-looking as they once were. They feel like they wear a badge that says "Relationship Loser," even though they look like winners to me. It is never too late to connect with The Right One. Understanding what you have to offer to a romantic partner is crucial to making that connection. Twenty-eight-year-old women don't feel as cute as they did at twenty-two—they start looking for their wrinkles; sixty-two-year-olds don't think they are as attractive as they were when they were forty. Yet, having survived a breakup gives you compassion as well as greater self-awareness. When you understand yourself better, you are more attractive to others. It's never too late! I know eighty-year-olds who have gotten married.

My job as a relationship coach is to help my reluctant clients who think they are over the hill to understand that their dread of going back out onto the dating scene is quite normal. Most everybody feels some anxiety when they are meeting someone new. My own husband claims that dating was not fun for him. When I coach, I ease my clients' fears by focusing on what my clients *do* have to offer in a relationship and by leaving very little to chance: preparing carefully for the date, choosing the right place to meet, making sure the clothes are just right, and preparing topics so the conversation flows easily. There are those coaching clients who feel down about themselves: the one who missed the boat with available men to date or the one who blew his chance with the last woman he dated…these clients require a perspective shift. Once they see these are all excuses to cover their fears, then it's possible, slowly and carefully, to build up their confidence, which will help them attract a new partner, no matter what their age.

♥ *Coach Amy's Dating Wisdom*

Instead of looking at rejection as a fearful, horrible occurrence and something to avoid, why not view it as a gift? Because of rejection, you will not waste your time with people who don't appreciate you. You are able to move on and invest your time and energy in a person who does value you. In this way, rejection is a gift.

Love and Marriage—and Children: How Long Should It Take?

Americans have a unique take on love and marriage. In a Rutgers University study, adults in Europe, Asia, and the United States were asked what the main purpose of marriage is. Seventy percent of the Americans (unlike all the others interviewed) said marriage was for the couple, not the children. Americans are also the only people who think it's wrong to stay in a bad marriage "for the sake of the children." Americans are clear-eyed about the role children play in a committed relationship. Children are at home for twenty years, not a big part of your life if you live until you are eighty, the current national average.

Women Over Thirty Who Want Children: A Timetable

For women in this age group who want children, the biological clock does matter. Today, many women over thirty-five are enhancing their fertility so they can have children later. However, later is not forever. Keep your goal of children in mind. Although it may be difficult, it is important to stay cool and focus on meeting the right man first.

Age	Time Frame	Follow-Up
For women 30–34 years old	Stay in a relationship only up to two years before expecting a commitment to the relationship or marriage, or move on.	It's probably a good idea to know your partner for at least eighteen months before marrying and starting a family.
For women 35–45 years old	Stay in a relationship for no more than a year before having your partner commit to children, or say goodbye.	After the wedding or commitment to a long-term relationship, start trying to conceive within six months.

The Role of Children in Your Get It Right Relationship

People who have children from previous relationships should factor in the children when they are making their plans with The Right One. Many people feel that having children is a disadvantage when dating, but that doesn't have to be.

I had a client who attended Parents Without Partners meetings because, though he didn't have children of his own, he liked children and wanted a relationship with a woman who already had kids. Children can also be a catalyst in a relationship, as they were for Richard and Brenda, two divorcees whose children were friends in school. Richard's daughter Christina and Brenda's daughter Jane enjoyed the weekends together when Richard had custody of Christina. The girls are officially stepsisters now.

When children from previous marriages are not already friends, give the relationship at least a full year, and perhaps two, before settling in. This will give all members of both families time to work out logistics and mesh households.

Women who do not want children may relax the time limits. It's up to you to be clear what you want from a relationship. Official walk-down-the-aisle marriage may not be what you and your partner want. If you already have children or don't want children, you might find a long-term exclusive relationship can be as satisfying as marriage. Some couples live in separate houses or even different cities. One person I coached, who was part of a couple, lived alone in a neighboring town from where the partner lived for the first twenty years of the relationship; then, the couple retired to Florida together. It all comes down to determining the situation you can live with and finding a partner who wants the same things. Marriage is not always the best model for people who love one another.

Men Who Want Families

In my research, among men from twenty-eight to fifty-seven, the desire to have a family is the number-one reason men get married. Their timetables are a little more relaxed than those of women with the same desire, but they still don't have all the time in the world. They need to keep the goal of family front and center.

Men in Their Thirties

Men in this age group are often focused on their careers. Marriage may not be a priority for them. Of course, as their careers evolve, so do their lifestyles and emotional needs. Relationships for men in this age group may or may not be headed toward marriage. The woman is usually the one who initiates the discussion of the future unless the man is Motivated to Marry™.

Age is less important in relationships than it used to be, but men have an issue with the biological clock, too! More important than age for men is maturity: being ready for the responsibility of marriage and a family. Today, many men (especially those who have professional degrees and live in urban centers) don't arrive at this point until they are in their late thirties.

Men in Their Forties

A man over forty-five who wants to find a partner has a much narrower pool to choose from if he also wants a family. I have men friends in their mid-forties who are considered "too old" by thirty-five-year-old women.

Still, many men like the comfort, the security, and the intimacy of an exclusive relationship, but they may not see it as leading to marriage. Another reason men marry is for companionship. They do not want to be alone. For instance, men who have lost their wives tend to marry again within two years of becoming widowers. This pull toward companionship is very strong.

Men in Their Fifties and Beyond

I see men in their fifties and sixties who think they want families. Yet, when they meet the right woman, they may be willing to give up that dream in exchange for the pleasures of marriage to her.

The right woman may have children already and may want no more or may have passed the childbearing years. For some men, "the pleasure of her company" is more valuable than the children they thought they wanted to have. They may also come to terms with the fact that raising children at this stage of life would be a difficult change of lifestyle.

Questions to Ask Yourself and Your Partner

You want to work these things out and make sure you avoid potential conflicts. Don't allow yourself to be totally seduced by the "happily ever after" scenario.

The Issue:	The Question	Another Question
Religion:	What	When
Sex:	When	How often
Living arrangements:	Where	When
Work schedules:	When	Where
Time together:	How much	When
Family time:	How much	When

The Issue:	either...	or
Commitment:	long-term relationship	marriage
Starting a family:	children	no children
Family:	more children	no more children

Seventy-five percent of couples who live together believe they will get married someday.

Again, both people need to have the same expectations and need to show respect for one another and each other's needs and desires. When you find that you don't want the same things at the same time, it is important to work toward negotiating these situations for a win/win solution where both parties feel their needs will be met—or the relationship will not survive.

Building a Future Together

Both people have to have the same expectations about the future and want a future together. That's a given. Once that is said, what does that future look like? Marriage? Family? Living in the same house or different houses? Will your kids be living with you as a couple full-time or part-time? Where will your vacations be? How will you spend the holidays—and with whom? What do you want to create together as a couple? It is very important to discuss your wants, needs, and expectations as individuals and as a couple. I am a big believer in couple counseling or coaching to ensure that you get all your issues on the table. When I got married for the second time, my husband-to-be and I went for coaching. I didn't want to leave any stone unturned. I wanted to go into this marriage with my eyes wide open.

What relationship skills can be improved? How are you at communicating with one another? How do you want to be (or behave) when life gets a bit topsy-turvy? What can you depend on your partner for when times get rough? All these things need to be discussed. Your goal is to Get It Right This Time™—so why not arm yourself with the knowledge, tools, and skills that will last you a lifetime?

I hope that this book will get you started thinking about the central relationship in your life. For too long, people have persisted in thinking that marriages are made in heaven and that love just happens. You have to make it happen. As Louis Pasteur, the great French doctor, said, "Chance favors the well-prepared." With this book as your guide, I wish you a safe and exciting journey into the world of love relationships.

—Amy

I wish I had the power to reach more people with the message you have just read. Why don't they teach these things in school? I feel so strongly that people should learn these concepts that I made Part VIII: *Dreams Come True Chapter* available free on my website. If you would like to share it with someone else—your friends, for example—just go to www.GetItRightThisTime.com and click on the free chapter link to download.

Afterword

Coach Amy's Personal Odyssey

Amy Schoen was born and raised in Longuyland in the New York City suburb of Valley Stream. She tried to lose her New York accent by going to Duke University (go, Blue Devils!) in North Carolina, but to no avail.

After a stint in Indianapolis, Indiana (she considered it "going abroad"), she came back East to earn an MBA at Georgetown University. She stayed in Washington, D.C., married her college sweetheart, and opened up her own women's clothing boutique in Bethesda, Maryland. The marriage lasted ten years while she operated the boutique for thirteen.

After the breakup of her first marriage, Amy became very active in the Washington-area singles scene. She also embarked on a journey of self-growth to learn what it takes to have a healthy, long-lasting relationship. This included research, coursework, counseling, and training. Amy left no stone unturned.

On a singles' biking trip, she met her present husband, Alan. They were engaged within six months and married within a year. Amy, Alan, and their mashugana cat Shayna live happily in Rockville, Maryland. Together, they enjoy dancing, skiing, tennis, and biking, as well as all the cultural gifts that D.C. has to offer.

Amy has followed her passion to help others by becoming a life coach. She created Heartmind Connection® as a multimedia approach to guiding others to more fulfilling relationships. Amy is fully living her career values by being an *independent, creative entrepreneur.* As she watches her clients reenter the world of dating after failed relationships, she enjoys the sense of being a *catalyst for positive change.* In *Get It Right This Time™,* she shares the secrets of starting over with positive intention and perseverance.

Amy Schoen is a popular speaker and the author of *Motivated to Marry™: A Better Method for Dating and Relationships* as well as *Thirty Very Good Reasons Not to Marry Until You Are Thirty.*

About HeartmindConnection.com

- Personal life and business coaching and consulting on dating and relationships
- One-on-one coaching
- Couples coaching
- Small group coaching

Amy Schoen has been transforming people to be their best for **more than twenty years.** She has the gift of visualization and uses it to help her clients visualize the kind of life they truly desire. To move her clients toward positive action, she draws upon her vast life and business experiences and keen knowledge of people. **Her clients have become more confident about themselves in the dating world and have developed a better sense of what they truly want in a relationship, leading them to successful relationships.**

Amy Schoen's Coaching Services

Amy Schoen helps improve your dating relationships through a method that clarifies what you truly need and want in a relationship, and supports you as you go out there to find it. Your search for committed, long-lasting love will become easier once you gain self-confidence by focusing on the special qualities you have to offer to a life partner.

Coach Amy Says:

Life coaching can help you start living the life you dream of today!

I cherish every client I work with. As your life coach, I help you discover your own special uniqueness. This will help you develop the self-confidence that will allow you to succeed in your search for committed love. Together, we create a safe space so you feel comfortable exploring what you really want for your life. I offer a custom-tailored approach to dating that takes into account your strengths, as well as your limitations, to determine what will work best for you.

Heartmind Connection® coaching is a whole life approach to dating relationships and is not a canned program! You will benefit from a blend of the self-discovery that is an outcome of life coaching with grounded, informative dating advice. Since your dating relationship impacts all areas of your life, you will be coached on all aspects of your life, working toward living a balanced life, as well as dealing with what's stopping you from getting what you truly want. Since life coaching is delivered via the telephone, you will be coached in the comfort of your own home or office!

I can help you be more successful in dating. You will:

- Gain a better understanding of yourself and your particular needs in a dating relationship. Then, you will be able to attract more ideal people to date.

- Increase your opportunities to meet more people, and choose better while dating, by honing in on shared values, life goals, and must-haves.

- Develop a greater sense of self-confidence.

- Become more aware of what you need in a dating relationship in order to be happy, and learn how to request it from your partner.

As a coach, I can help you solve the following problems:

- Feeling more in control of the dating process. You will avoid haphazard dating.
- Finding where to put your best energy for meeting the right kind of person who will give you the greatest chance of success.
- Helping you gain more balance in your life so you have more time to do the things you love.
- Gaining clarity on whether you should stay in your current relationship or move on.
- Learning what personal characteristics are necessary in a partner in order to ensure lasting bliss—this time!

Read my coaching testimonials online at www.Heartmind Connection.com.

Are you:

- Feeling frustrated with the singles dating scene?
- Not dating because you are not sure how to begin again or have just given up?
- Constantly running around to singles events trying to meet The One with little or no result?
- Staying in a relationship much too long before realizing it is going nowhere?
- Allowing yourself to become complacently satisfied with the status quo and yet knowing deep down you want more out of life?

Save time, energy, and money by coaching with Amy. Together you will work on Getting It Right This Time!

Don't forget to go to www.HeartmindConnection.com to receive the free monthly e-zine with helpful dating and relationship articles and updated resources that will help you in your search for your ideal life partner.

Coach Amy helps you connect with yourself more fully so you can connect with others more successfully.

Resources

Everybody thinks love is just something that happens to people. Nothing could be further from the truth. You will increase your chances of finding love by surfing the dating sites listed below to learn what's available to you. Additional sites are added regularly to my website at www.HeartmindConnection.com.

You will also want to spend some time learning more about yourself. Books and CDs listed here present insights about relationships that will be very helpful to you. With these resources, you can view your search for a mate not as a desperate quest but as a fun learning experience and a journey into personal growth.

Online Dating Sites

Here are some top online dating websites where my clients and friends have had success in finding significant love relationships. Before you try your hand at writing your online dating profile, read my articles provided on my web page:

www.HeartmindConnection.com

Also, I can help you write your Internet dating profile to attract the right person to you. This list is a good start and not at all exhaustive. Please check the Resources area on my website to see the latest sites that have been added. There is definitely something for everyone!

- *AnimalAttraction.com:* A dating website for pet owners and admirers. There are subscribers in all fifty states. Female to male ratio is three-to-one. My husband had to pass *the cat test* when we were dating! www.animalattraction.com

- *Big Beautiful Women Personals Plus:* This site is for women who are voluptuous and men who appreciate that. www.bbwpersonalsplus.com

- *Blacksingles.com:* An online community created specifically for African-American singles to make new friends or to find a life-long partner who shares similar values, traditions, and beliefs. www.blacksingles.com

- *Christian Café:* Several of my Christian friends really like this site and have met nice people. www.ChristianCafe.com

- *Classical Music Lovers' Exchange:* For unattached music lovers since 1980. I know a woman who had good experiences with this site in New York City and met great people. www.cmle.com

- *Cycling Singles:* An online matchmaking service that connects you with other cycling enthusiasts. Posting a photo and searching are free. www.cyclingsingles.com

- *eHarmony:* Since the process of signing up is very time-consuming, it attracts a serious person who really wants to find his or her soul mate. It seems harder to make a connection, but when you do, your chances are better than average that it might work out. This company has been advertising a ton. eHarmony.com

- *Fitness Singles:* An online dating service that pairs people according to their interest in more than seventy activities from badminton to yoga. Posting profiles and searching are free, but sending an email requires a monthly membership fee. www.fitnesssingles.com

- *Frumster:* An Internet dating site devoted to traditional and observant Jewish singles who are marriage-minded. There is a careful screening process that requires members to be sincere and serious. Lying will not be tolerated, and there is a screening process to ensure complete integrity for all members. www.frumster.com

- *JDate:* A popular international Jewish dating site. I personally know several couples who have met on this site. Many of my friends have been utilizing this site to meet a mate. They also have parties in major cities where singles can get together, face-to-face. www.JDate.com

- *JMatch.com:* A new, up-and-coming site for Jewish singles. The jury is still out! www.JMatch.com

- *Match.com:* One of the largest sites for meeting singles. It accommodates different faiths and sexual preferences. I know couples who have met from this site and are now married. www.Match.com

- *Planet Out:* A dating website for the lesbian community. I have clients who have liked this site. www.Planetout.com

- *Right Stuff Dating:* An international introduction service that puts singles from select (Ivy plus) universities in touch with one another through a newsletter and the Internet. www.Rightstuffdating.com

- *Saw You at Sinai:* This site is oriented toward Jewish singles and combines traditional matchmaking with modern technology. You can choose your own matchmaker to search and find the right match for you. There is more privacy here since only potential matches suggested by your matchmaker can see your profile. www.sawyouatsinai.com

- *Single Parent Match:* Here is a site that hooks up single parents with each other or someone who wouldn't mind meeting a single parent. The site has resources for single parents as well. www.singleparentmatch.com

- *Soulmatch:* An online dating service focused on values, faith, and the search for spiritual chemistry. You are able to search for matches of the same faith. www.Soulmatch.com

- *Spiritual Singles:* This is the site for singles who are spiritually oriented with no particular religious affiliation. It is highly recommended by my spiritual friends. www.spiritualsingles.com

- *Truedater.com:* A site that allows you to share reviews of whether the information in a person's online dating profile is true or not. This site should keep people honest! www.truedater.com

- *Where Christians Meet:* A Christian dating site that screens members to make sure they are real. Oriented toward "serious" singles. It requires a $25,000 minimum income to be a member. www.wherechristiansmeet.com

- *World Singles:* An international dating site that offers various nationalities or niche communities to choose from—from Greek to Arabs to Black singles. www.worldsingles.com

- *Yahoo Personals:* An everyone and anyone site. It's up to you to screen who you choose to meet. The site promotes a SmartFit™ matching system; you must take a relationship test to qualify for its Premier dating service. www.personals.yahoo.com

Special Interest Groups for Singles

If you want to meet someone in your neighborhood, go to my website's Resources page at www.HeartmindConnection.com/resources.html for a listing of groups in particular major cities.

Divorced Individuals

Are you ready to get out there and meet people after a divorce? There are very supportive dating and singles groups specifically for divorced individuals in your area that help with dating after divorce. It's helpful to be around those who understand where you are coming from and who are dealing with the same issues.

- *Parents Without Partners (PWP):* A wonderful organization for divorced people with children offering support and friendship. There are local area chapters. They have a variety of events with and without the children. www.parentswithoutpartners.org

Singles Travel Groups and Vacation Spots

- *Backroads:* Biking, hiking, and active trips. Worldwide singles + solo trips oriented toward people traveling by themselves. My husband Alan went biking in France with this group. He still has their old ratty T-shirt! www.backroads.com

- *Carnival Cruise Line:* This cruise line is more casual and tends to attract more singles. www.carnivalcruise.com

- *Club Med:* All-inclusive resort clubs all around the world. You can search for an all-adult club or one with facilities and activities for children. Wide age ranges. Certain clubs are known for singles' crowds. I went with a singles' group to Turks and Caicos. Cancun is another very singles-oriented location. www.clubmed.com

- *Contiki:* For those ages eighteen to thirty-five. Tours that travel worldwide with an emphasis on European destinations and some U.S. tours. Some resort locations too! www.contiki.com

- *Kripalu Center*, Lenox, MA: A weekend retreat for yoga and discussion. www.kripalu.org

- *Marion Smith Travel:* Organizes weekends, offering cruises and active trips for singles within the U.S. and the Caribbean. www.marionsmithtravel.com

- *Steppin' Out Adventures:* From skiing trips to horseback riding, Steppin' Out Adventures hosts an array of exciting adventures, both in America and internationally. The group is incorporating at least one service day in its itinerary to give participants an opportunity to interact with local people and to give back to the country they are visiting. Steppin' Out specializes in adventures for singles. www.steppinoutadventures.com

- *Sundancer Cruises:* Cruises all over the world that feature dancing and dance lessons with top instructors. About half of the cruise is singles, with average ages in the forties and fifties. www.sundancercruises.net

Jewish Singles

- *Amazing Journeys:* Jewish singles travel all around the world. Sponsored by the JCC of Pittsburgh. www.amazingjourneys.net

- *American Jewish Congress:* Singles trips that go all over the world. This is a high-class group with wonderful accommodations and tour guides. I traveled several times with this group. Average age is mid-thirties with range of 29–49. Since it is based in New York City, it draws heavily from the East Coast. www.ajcongress travel.com

- *Basherte:* Spiritual weekends for Jewish singles with activities and workshops to form close-knit connections. www.basherte.org

- *Jewish Singles Vacations:* Well-priced trips that travel both in the U.S. and abroad. Sam will get you there, but you need to do much of the research of what to do on your own. Bring several good guidebooks. Both Alan and I traveled with this group—at different times! www.tourgroups.com/jsv

- *JSinglesCruise.com:* Cruises organized for Jewish singles in two age groups: 20–40 and 40–60. The group claims to have equal ratios of men and women. www.jsinglescruise.com

- *Mosaic Outdoors (Mountain) Clubs of America:* A network of nonprofit organizations dedicated to organizing outdoor and environmental activities for Jewish singles, couples, and families. There are more than twenty-five clubs located throughout the United States, Canada, and Israel. Mosaic serves Jews of all ages, both married and single, who share a love of nature and the outdoors. I have been on their national ski trips. www.mosaics.org

- *United Jewish Singles Alliance.* Mostly thirties (and I'm sure forties, too!) travel within the U.S. and worldwide. None of my friends have been on one of these trips, so I have no information. Offers singles trips for non-Jews as well. www.UJSA.com

Online Dating Directories

You have just hit the mother lode. These directories of online dating websites have lists and lists of resources pertaining to dating and singles from dating personals to dating advice about relationship issues.

- *LuvSource.com:* A dating online personals directory that includes dating services and various online dating sites with travel and entertainment information, dating advice, and gifts to purchase. www.luvsource.com

- *Singles On The Go:* A list of many singles groups and online resources by niche and geographical area. It is very comprehensive! www.singlesonthego.com

- *www.AmazingSingles.com:* Tons of information for singles by geographic location. I especially like the event listings. Also, the site has links to top personal sites, travel information, and other resources for singles. www.amazingsingles.com

- *www.AskGrannyDate.com:* Provides relevant up-to-date online dating information for people who are looking into online dating. The site reviews and grades the online dating experience. Also, dating articles are provided FYI. www.AskGrannyDate.com

- *www.1st-Dating-Tips.com:* All sorts of website resources for dating tips. www.1st-Dating-Tips.com

- *www.LoveCompass.com:* A single source for online personals, online dating services, singles, love, romance, matchmaking, and dating services agencies on one website. It also has a directory of websites related to singles, relationships, travel, dating personals, etc. www.LoveCompass.com

- *www.Online-Dating.org:* An online dating directory with personals and matchmaking directory, chatrooms, speed-dating sites, and advice articles. www.Online-Dating.org

- *www.SinglesBrowser.com:* Has several online dating services and lists local singles events, such as speed dating, by region. Also has a dating advice library and other fun and interesting information. www.SinglesBrowser.com

- *www.thematematcher.com:* A wonderful resource with connections to the most poplar online dating sites. They also have articles, tips, gifts and extras to give you the tools needed for your dating success.

Books

These are some of my favorites and others that have been recommended to me.

Are You the One for Me? by Barbara De Angelis, Ph.D. (1992)

Authentic Happiness by Martin Seligman, Ph.D. (2002)

Before You Say "I Do" by Todd Outcalt (1998)

Body Language Secrets: A Guide During Courtship and Dating by R. Don Steele (1999)

Conscious Dating: Finding the Love of Your Life in Today's World by David Steele (2006)

The Conscious Heart by Kathlyn Hendricks, Ph.D., and Gay Hendricks, Ph.D. (1997)

Date or Soul Mate? How to Know If Someone Is Worth Pursuing in Two Dates or Less by Neil Clark Warren (2005)

Facing the Facts: The Truth about Sex and You by Brenna Jones and Stan Jones (2007)

The Five Love Languages for Singles by Gary Chapman (2004)

The Four Agreements by Don Miguel Ruiz (2001)

How to Get a Date Worth Keeping: Be Dating in Six Months or Your Money Back by Henry Cloud (2005)

How to Succeed with Men by David Copeland (2005)

If You Really Loved Me: 101 Questions on Dating, Relationships, and Sexual Purity by Jason Evert (2003)

Keeping the Love You Find by Harville Hendrix, Ph.D. (1992)

Love Smart: Find the One You Want—Fix the One You Got by Dr. Phil McGraw (2006)

Mars and Venus on a Date by John Gray, Ph.D. (1997)

Men Are from Mars, Women Are from Venus by John Gray, Ph.D. (1992)

More Than a Match: How to Turn the Dating Game into Lasting Love by Michael Smalley (2007)

Negotiating Love by Riki Robbins Jones, Ph.D. (1995)

1001 Ways to Be Romantic by Greg Godek (1995)

The Right Relationship Can Happen: How to Create Relationship Success by Nancy Lynn Pina (2000)

The Shy Single: A Bold Guide to Dating for the Less-Than-Bold Dater by Bonnie Jacobson and Sandra J. Gordon (2004)

Think Like a Guy: How to Get a Guy by Thinking Like One by Giuliana Depandi (2006)

Transitions by William Bridges (1980)

Why Marriages Succeed or Fail by John Gottman, Ph.D. (1994)

CDs

Be prepared with a body of knowledge on how to make the most of your significant love relationship with these CDs and other educational products. Learn to be an expert on Internet dating, romance, and finessing relationship issues.

Boundaries in Dating: Making Dating Work by Dr. Henry Cloud and Dr. John Townsend (2006)

Conscious Dating for Relationship Success: How to Find the Love of Your Life and The Life That You Love by David Steele (2005)

Create Loving Relationships: Using Creative Visualization to Attract Your Soul Mate by Sound Experience (1997)

Men Are from Mars, Women Are from Venus Interactive Workshop on CD-ROM by M2K (CD-ROM) (2004)

Modern Dating Tips by Jensen Bell (2005)

97 Secrets to a Happy Relationship by pushbutton (CD-ROM, 2004)

12 Stages of Romantic Relationship by Gregory Morgan (2004)

Other Resources

- *Compass Life Designs:* A wealth of information for all areas of your life from a team of expert coaches. See my weekly blog as the site's relationship expert. www.compasslifedesigns.com

- *SelfGrowth.com:* Tons of articles and resources from top self-growth gurus. It is the #1 personal growth site. My articles are listed there. www.selfgrowth.com

- *www.55-Alive.com:* A resource for adults over fifty who are exploring the next phase of their life. I do a monthly Q&A column on relationships. www.55-alive.com

Index